Ascension through Love

Kendra Farmer

BookLeaf Publishing

Presentation by *BookLeaf Publishing*

Web: www.bookleafpub.com

E-mail: info@bookleafpub.com

ISBN: 9789357210935

First edition 2022

DEDICATION

I dedicated this book to my children. As the saying goes, when a woman needs true love she is gifted a son. I aspire to keep the twinkle in your eyes, my sweet baby boys.

ACKNOWLEDGEMENT

I am grateful for all the genuine love I gave
witness to in my life. I am thankful that in each
season of my life I knew love based on how it
felt and how it was delivered. I want to
recognize my mother for being an avid supporter
of my writing. She continues to buy me
notebooks and supports my pen-to-paper writing
style. The same style that helped me curate my
first anthology of poems.

PREFACE

Writing has always been my deepest and most genuine form of expression. Poetry was one of the first artist writing forms that fascinated me. The way words carry weight and paint timeless pictures is a surreal experience for me. Thumbing through the notes of my life, I found art and messages inscribed in the margin. The poems were written in high school notebooks and college binders, this anthology came to fruition as I attempted to capture energy in motion on paper. Each poem was written in a different decade in my life. From sunrise to sunset, you can trace the understanding of love as I aged through the years. My only hope is that these words resonate with other individuals and help make sense of this beautiful journey that is life.

Nature's Kiss

Full delectable, yet delicate lips
Curled around a sweet center
Intimacy dripping from every crevice
Enticing body, full of wonder
The enigma that holds nature
So facetious in the action
the organic way you express love
so succinct and astounding
the wind blows, your body moans
the sun shines, you come alive
It's like watching nature
intimate with elusive beings
Provocative lips pouted
--Devilishly colored
Giving into unspoken wishes
Incognito is your style
Impetuous creation
Everywhere I look, I see this kiss
Feathered flights caressing the sky
Serenading crickets on a summer night
Nature is never quiescent
Always loving...always kissing

Hurricane

I want that swift kind of love
the kind that comes
engulfs me whole
pulling me down into a torrent
carrying me, wave after wave
away to the other side of an island
where the native tongue is understanding

I want that deep kind of love
where the brightest ray couldn't shed light
and the soul is the holy being that knows without
sight
within these depths
no teaching, all knowing
where the native delicacy is trust

I want the pure kind of love
the kind the mind cant comprehend
but the heart understands
profession made from a place of yearning
nevermore alone
and the native thought is longing

levels to lonely

3

life without love
is lived in darkness
love possesses a flame
that illuminates the abyss
captures in every empty heart
surrounded by a field of dreams
unmet and unfulfilled, life without love
is a life full of pain knowing there a half
unobtained

Life is Love

Loving is easy
because it can't be stopped
Trusting is hard
because it requires thought
Knowing is wanting
a peaceful mine
Acting is unnerving
to a heart that's blind
Letting go is vexing
while holding on is hexing
The more you live,
the more you love.
The more your love,
the more you hurt.
The more your hurt,
the more you learn.
The more you learn,
the more you grow.
But then you'll know
That life is love is pain is hurt is rain, so don't be
afraid to grow.
Live for now for this too shall pass.
Yesterday is gone, time to leave it in the past.

09/4/2007

Untouchable

The longing and taunting
of me wanting you.
There is sorrow and dread
as I'm thrown askew.
I want you. Do you love me?
But we do not belong
for we dance to different songs.
You have your own
but you say you're done.
You ask me why not,
you claim we are one.
The truth is simple,
you belong to another.

Questions for my lover..

Can you love me with your whole heart, and not
just the selfish part?
I need to be the first soul you crave morning,
noon, and night.
I don't want to be a burden when I need time and
affection.
Can you love me with your whole body, not just
the kinky part?
Use all five of your senses, to break me into
pieces.
Find all the good and the bad, and make it your
perfection.
Can you love me with your whole mind, the art
and analytical?
Get inside, learn what makes me.
Leaving behind deception, and finding the things
I choose not to show.
Can I know the real you and give my heart a
chance?
To choose my lover

Echo

Compelled by the power of a kiss.
Is
To always strive and never quit.
It
Your soul came in and entrapped me cruelly.
Truly
Within a year, same day...or hour
Our
With you, my ego slept in so late.
Fate
I was filled with rage, yet still received you.
To
Swiftness, a cunning a couldn't believe.
Be?
You came along with such tenderness.
This,
Questions rising, why should I be blessed?
you and me
With this love shared between us,
is
It is intricate and profound
found in
Leaving thoughts and longing to be a wife.
life

Being there for you each and every day
very
Exuberant and shunning the fear, no longer
scared.   rarely.

Love letters

Increasing ambitions for what we have.
Willing to do anything to make you laugh.
I want to be involved in all that you do.
Leaving you is an option I'd never pursue.
Living my life with the man I love
Little acronym, a love poem for you.
Only God knows how much you make me soar.
Very small things you do show me gratitude.
Every moment of the day, I long to see your
face.
You possess everything I want in a man.
Overwhelming joy is what I feel when I think of
you.
Untreatable feeling, a sort of knee weakness and
butterflies.
Addicted to your taste and the strength of your
hands.
Loving the way you devour my thoughts and
kisses.
When I lay my head I pray over your heart.
And I revel in the joy you impart.
You got me sprung in the worst way
Silly thoughts of you continue to bless my day.

It goes without saying, I will love you always.

10

My heart your home

a place you can go
to cleanse your mind
and free your soul
if ever you're in need
simply come home to me
my heart is your home
lay your head on my chest
relax your mind and get some rest
do you hear that melody
that song my body plays
it's a familiar rhythm
you're addicted to its waves
don't ever stray too far from here
your true love resides near
cause my heart is your home
from this life to the next

elephant in the room

the central force behind this life we possess
will be the same force that detonates this bomb
it will eventually blow us apart, shattering
reality
it will all come crashing down, exposing little
things
the secret ingredient to our seemingly perfect
recipe
as we sift through the debris we will find the
pieces
that never truly fit together, the ones that always
hurt to touch
so we left the unfiled, now debris in a pile
left untouched to grow, unchecked
into vile little monsters with no remorse or
regret

a misunderstanding

Can you hear my heart breaking?
I can feel all the scary changes
taking place in our lonely souls
at one point I thought this was love
now glamorless, it is clear it was lust
Can you hear me now?
Because my heart misunderstood.

Losing you

I am losing you
like a feather loses its way
flying on the wind
moving on words unspoken
I am losing you
like sand through folded hands
returning to the land
I am losing you
I feel it in everything
from the moments not together
the absent kisses on my lips
like a winter day
so bitter and short
I can hear it, I see it, I feel it.
I am losing you.

Woman Enough

I am reflecting back on a love gone wrong
A love that scraped me and raped me.
Took from me what I thought was being a
woman.
Left me curled in a ball crying.
Praying that he would come back to me.
Save me, from the hell he built for me.
He escaped from the clutches of love.
Left me standing here holding the ball.
Deceived me into believing his love was given.
But left me empty and covered in wounds and
weapons.
Now I am wondering if I am woman enough to
trust again.
Surely I can't trust myself and judgment past this
pain.
Find someone, and believe they'll show me
honesty.
Giving from his soul, the love that he knows.
Give him me, completely without hesitation.
Leave me open for another failure.
The past left me dreaming of a day
when I would be woman enough.
But still wondering about love. Surely he exists.
A man strong enough to untangle me.

Lay me naked for all my pain and secrets to be
seen.
Without pain or physical gain,
with a truth that is his and a faith grown from
seeds.
Reap and sowed into the love for women that is
expressed as protection.

Touching Stones

Cold slabs, hard jabs
Filled with doubt; chasing clout
Forehead kisses, cheek caresses
Building bridges while jumping fences
Warm blankets and late talks
Unwinding mysteries on long walks.
The inevitable attachment
Unbridled commitment
Is love possible when touching stones?
Walls built after moments long gone.
Worries and fears brewing a tea of denial.
The hope of a future clouded in doubt
Projecting tears into accusations and
misinterpretations.
As a delusion of love destroys your chances to
grow.
Denying desires because of unrealistic
expectations.
Cold and damp rocks want nothing more than to
be touched stones.

Empty

I sit here contemplating and deliberating
On how I am going to give you something
I clearly do not possess
You see, I would love to be with you
But I am clueless as to how
Why make such a vow
When I am empty inside
My essence was drained
From my soul to my mind
a part of me is gone
Lost from a love gone wrong
It came from the left
Taking a part of me with it
That same it,
That made me... me
We could surely be a we
If only I weren't empty
I am not saying I am shallow
Simply that my shell is hollow
If I were able to show you that warmth
Possessed deep within a woman's hearth
I would love to transport you there
To a state of being when I wasn't so empty.

Playground Love

Wish I could go back to that playground love
back when you slipped a simple note
filled with only a few words and two boxes
and you anticipated check marks
that is when loving was so much easier
anxious all day for us to go play
so we could sneak kisses behind slides
but in front of our friends our love we hide
you'd pull my hair, I would push you down.
and that was a simple expression on the
playground.
too bad we can't go back to that
a simpler time for love
when signals were never mixed
but sometimes expressed our love with this
and made up for it with candy kisses
oh how I miss that playground love
when outside factors mattered the least
what happened yesterday was a thing of the past
that's when you truly knew the love was pure
when I was yours and you were mine
And love only knew games because of recess
time.

Armageddon

Letting you in was not part of the plan
You were not supposed to be all in my head
Invading my mind and stealing my heart
I have heard love was painful
Never thought my mom would be right
My love for you is very well known
It flows deeper, down to my soul
But there are times I need to be alone
Love you is unshaped and without thought
Completely without rhyme or reason
I am torn between this passion for you
And my hearts will shut you out
Subtle words increase the anxiety
Do not hurt me. Please don't destroy me.
Since you have invaded my paradise.

Swiper

He swiped me, this night thief
His tunnel vision saw right through me
One phone call ran through it all
Said it right; kept it tight
Full of rapture, the thrill was right
One those hours of vexing moments
Timid touches and lazy kisses
These haunting frames, a dangerous game.
Swiping souls and taking names.
Empty vessels with golden treasures.
Judgment clouded by the stormy weather
Sharing pain while robbing peace.
This swiper swiped every part of me.

Addressing My Soul

What is wrong? what is wrong?
Your heart is sad and downcast.
Reflecting an aura confused and trouble.
What is wrong girl? What is wrong?
That little girl no longer plays.
She sits inside by the window all day.
What is wrong dreamer? What is wrong?
The belletrist is lost for words.
While she puts all her dreams on hold.
What is wrong little star? What is wrong?
No longer are your eyes bright or jovial.
Your distance and telling of pain.
What is wrong? What is missing?
My sweet soul what is wrong with you?

Beautiful Storm

Filled with rage
The grace of a butterfly
Masking all the anger
With a cloud of raining beauty
Batted wings thrash lands afar
With gusts of wind
Full of leaves and sand
Floating in these silent waves
Perched on stems of eternal life
With mighty legs
This weightless storm
Ripping away innocence
Exposing intent behind love
Emerging from a state of destruction
A brand new place, a healed creation

Queen,

a title that was inherited not just from my
mother,
but from our legacy.
a story not written in ink, but scribed in blood
and tears
shed over years of turmoil.
it was never drafted on any degradable
parchment,
instead, it was engraved on the minds
of those who valued women.
an open heart and a strong will were considered
a gift,
with no death sentence to her soul.
poise enough to heel a man, she resonated with
grace
as her power swept the land.
this era existed before the ignorant imitators
 blurred the lines and erased the standards.
a true queen cannot be recognized by her title,
she uplifts nations with her works.
liberally freeing herself of ignorance .
Never shrinking herself,
or diminishing the next person's shine.
emitting an aura, radiating beauty from her core
she is the alpha and omega, the now and before.